Applied Psychology: Driving Power of Thought

By Warren Hilton

CONTENTS

Chapter Page

I. JUDICIAL MENTAL OPERATIONS

VITALIZING INFLUENCE OF CERTAIN IDEAS 3 WORK OF PRINCE, GERRISH, SIDIS, JANET, BINET 4 THE TWO TYPES OF THOUGHT 5

II. CAUSAL JUDGMENTS

ELEMENTARY CONCLUSIONS 9 FIRST EFFORT OF THE MIND 10 DISTORTED EYE PICTURES 11 ELEMENTS THAT MAKE UP AN IDEA 12 CAUSAL JUDGMENTS AND THE OUTER WORLD 13

III. CLASSIFYING JUDGMENTS

THE MARVEL OF THE MIND 17 THE INDELIBLE IMPRESS 18 HOW IDEAS ARE CREATED 19 THE ARCHIVES OF THE MIND 22

IV. THE FOUR PRIME LAWS OF ASSOCIATION

THE SEEMING CHAOS OF MIND 27 PREDICTING YOUR NEXT IDEA 28 THE BONDS OF INTELLECT 29 BRANDS AND TAGS 32 HOW EXPERIENCE IS SYSTEMATIZED 33 HOW LANGUAGE IS SIMPLIFIED 34 PROCESSES OF REASONING AND REFLECTION 35

V. EMOTIONAL ENERGY IN BUSINESS

IDEAS THAT STIMULATE 39 PIVOTAL LAW OF BUSINESS PASSION 40 ENERGIZING EMOTIONS 41 CROSS-ROADS OF SUCCESS OR FAILURE 42 THE LIFE OF EFFORT 43 THE MOTIVE POWER OF PROGRESS 44 THE VALUE OF AN IDEA 45 THE HARD WORK REQUIRED TO FAIL 46 CREATIVE POWER OF THOUGHT 47

CONSCIOUS AND UNCONSCIOUS TRAINING 48 TWO WAYS OF ATTACKING BUSINESS PROBLEMS 49 CUTTING INTO THE QUICK 50 EXECUTIVES, REAL AND SHAM 51 MENTAL ATTITUDE OF ONE'S BUSINESS 52 PSYCHOLOGICAL ENGINEERING 53

VI. HOW TO SELECT EMPLOYEES

A CLUE TO ADAPTABILITY 57 MAPPING THE MENTALITY 58 THE KIND OF "HELP" YOU NEED 59 TESTS FOR DIFFERENT MENTAL TRAITS 60 TEST OF UNCONTROLLED ASSOCIATIONS 61 TEST FOR QUICK THINKING 62 MEASURING SPEED OF THOUGHT 63 RANGE OF MENTAL TESTS 64 TESTS FOR ARMY AND NAVY 65 TESTS FOR RAILROAD EMPLOYEES 66 WHAT ONE FACTORY SAVED 67 PROFESSOR MUSTERBERG'S EXPERIMENTS 68 TESTS FOR HIRING TELEPHONE GIRLS 69 MEMORY TEST 71 TEST FOR ATTENTION 72 TEST FOR GENERAL INTELLIGENCE 74 TEST FOR EXACTITUDE 76 TEST FOR RAPIDITY OF MOVEMENT 77 TEST FOR ACCURACY OF MOVEMENT 78 RESULTS OF EXPERIMENTS 79 THEORY AND PRACTICE 85 HOW TO IDENTIFY THE UNFIT 87 MEANS TO GREAT BUSINESS ECONOMIES 88 ROUND PEGS IN SQUARE HOLES 89 THE DANGER IN TWO-FIFTHS OF A SECOND 90 PICKING A PRIVATE SECRETARY 91 FINDING OUT THE CLOSE-MOUTHED 92 A TEST FOR SUGGESTIBILITY 93 SELECTING A STENOGRAPHER 95 TESTS FOR AUDITORY ACUITY 96 A TEST FOR ROTE MEMORY 97 A TEST FOR RANGE OF VOCABULARY 100 CRIME-DETECTION BY PSYCHOLOGICAL TESTS 105 THE FACTORY OPERATIVE'S ATTENTION POWER 106 KINDS OF TESTING APPARATUS 108 ANALYSIS OF DIFFERENT CALLINGS 109 EXERCISES FOR DEVELOPING SPECIAL FACULTIES 110 PRINCIPLES THAT BEAR ON PRACTICAL AFFAIRS 111

CHAPTER I

JUDICIAL MENTAL OPERATIONS

[Sidenote: Vitalizing Influence of Certain Ideas]

One of the greatest discoveries of modern times is the impellent energy of thought.

That every idea in consciousness is energizing and carries with it an impulse to some kind of muscular activity is a comparatively new but well-settled principle of psychology. That this principle could be made to serve practical ends seems never to have occurred to anyone until within the last few years.

[Sidenote: The Work of Prince, Gerrish, Sidis, Janet, Binet]

Certain eminent pioneers in therapeutic psychology, such men as Prince, Gerrish, Sidis, Janet, Binet and other physician-scientists, have lately made practical use of the vitalizing influence of certain classes of ideas in the healing of disease.

We shall go farther than these men have gone and show you that the impellent energy of ideas is the means to all practical achievement and to all practical success.

Preceding books in this Course have taught that--

I. All human achievement comes about through some form of bodily activity.

II. All bodily activity is caused, controlled and directed by the mind.

III. The mind is the instrument you must employ for the accomplishment of any purpose.

[Sidenote: The Two Types of Thought]

You have learned that the fundamental processes of the mind are the Sense-

Perceptive Process and the Judicial Process.

So far you have considered only the former--that is to say, sense-impressions and our perception of them. You have learned through an analysis of this process that the environment that prescribes your conduct and defines your career is wholly mental, the product of your own selective attention, and that it is capable of such deliberate molding and adjustment by you as will best promote your interests.

But the mere perception of sense-impressions, though a fundamental part of our mental life, is by no means the whole of it. The mind is also able to look at these perceptions, to assign them a meaning and to reflect upon them. These operations constitute what are called the Judicial Processes of the Mind.

The Judicial Processes of the Mind are of two kinds, so that, in the last analysis, there are, in addition to sense-perceptions, two, and only two, types of thought.

One of these types of thought is called a Causal Judgment and the other a Classifying Judgment.

CHAPTER II

CAUSAL JUDGMENTS

A Causal Judgment interprets and explains sense-perceptions. For instance, the tiny baby's first vague notion that something, no knowing what, must have caused the impressions of warmth and whiteness and roundness and smoothness that accompany the arrival of its milk-bottle--this is a causal judgment.

[Sidenote: Elementary Conclusions]

The very first conclusion that you form concerning any sensation that reaches you is that something produced it, though you may not be very clear as to just what that something is. The conclusions of the infant mind, for example, along this line must be decidedly vague and indefinite, probably going no further than to determine that the cause is either inside or outside of the body. Even then its judgment may be far from sure.

[Sidenote: First Effort of the Mind]

Yet, baby or grown-up, young or old, the first effort of every human mind upon the receipt and perception of a sensation is to find out what produced it. The conclusion as to what did produce any particular sensation is plainly enough a judgment, and since it is a judgment determining the cause of the sensation, it may well be termed a causal judgment.

Causal judgments, taken by themselves, are necessarily very indefinite. They do not go much beyond deciding that each individual sensation has a cause, and is not the result of chance on the one hand nor of spontaneous brain excitement on the other. Taken by themselves, causal judgments are disconnected and all but meaningless.

[Sidenote: Distorted Eye Pictures]

I look out of my window at the red-roofed stone schoolhouse across the way, and, so far as the eye-picture alone is concerned, all that I get is an impression of a flat, irregularly shaped figure, part white and part red. The image has but two dimensions, length and breadth, being totally lacking in depth or perspective. It is a flat, distorted, irregular outline of two of the four sides of the building. It is not at all like the big solid masonry structure in which a thousand children are at work. My causal judgments trace this eye-picture to its source, but they do not add the details of distance, perspective, form and size, that distinguish the reality from an architect's front elevation. These causal judgments of visual perceptions must be associated and compared with others before a real "idea" of the schoolhouse can come to me.

[Sidenote: Elements that Make Up an Idea]

Taken by themselves, then, causal judgments fall far short of giving us that truthful account of the outside world which we feel that our senses can be depended on to convey.

[Sidenote: Causal Judgments and the Outer World]

If there were no mental processes other than sense-perceptions and causal judgments, every man's mind would be the useless repository of a vast collection of facts, each literally true, but all without arrangement, association or utility. Our notion of what the outside world is like would be very different from what it is. We would have no concrete "ideas" or conceptions, such as "house," "book," "table," and so on. Instead, all our "thinking" would be merely an unassorted jumble of simple, disconnected sense-perceptions.

What, then, is the process that unifies these isolated sense-perceptions and gives us our knowledge of things as concrete wholes?

CHAPTER III

CLASSIFYING JUDGMENTS

[Sidenote: The Marvel of the Mind]

A Classifying Judgment associates and compares present and past sense-perceptions. It is the final process in the production of that marvel of the mind, the "idea."

The simple perception of a sensation unaccompanied by any other mental process is something that never happens to an adult human being.

In the infant's mind the arrival of a sense-impression arouses only a perception, a consciousness of the sense-impression. In the mind of any other person it awakens not only this present consciousness but also the associated memories of past experiences.

[Sidenote: The Indelible Impress]

Upon the slumbering mind of the newborn babe the very first message from the sense-organs leaves its exquisite but indelible impress. The next sense-perception is but part of a state of consciousness, in which the memory of the first sense-perception is an active factor. This is a higher type of mental activity. It is a something other and more complex than the mere consciousness of a sensory message and the decision as to its source.

The moment, then, that we get beyond the first crude sense-perception consciousness consists not of detached sensory images but of "ideas," the complex product of present sense-perceptions, past sense-perceptions and the mental processes known to psychology as association and discrimination.

[Sidenote: How Ideas are Created]

Every concrete conception or idea, such as "horse," "rose," "mountain," is made up of a number of associated properties. It has mass, form and various degrees of color, light and shade. Every quality it possesses is represented by a corresponding visual, auditory, tactual or other sensation.

Thus, your first sense-perception of coffee was probably that of sight. You perceived a brown liquid and your causal judgment explained that this sense-perception was the result of something outside of your body. Standing alone, this causal judgment meant very little to you, so far as your knowledge of coffee was concerned. So also the causal judgment that traced your sense of the smell of coffee to some object in space meant little until it was added to and associated with your eye-vision of that same point in space. And it was only when the causal judgment explaining the taste of coffee was added to the other two that you had an "idea" of what coffee really was.

When you look at a building, you receive a number and variety of simultaneous sensations, all of which, by the exercise of a causal judgment, you at once ascribe to the same point in space. From this time on the same flowing together of sensations from the same place will always mean for you that particular material thing, that particular building. You have a sensation of yellow, and forthwith a causal judgment tells you that something outside of your body produced it. But it would be a pretty difficult matter for you to know just what this something might be if there were not other simultaneous sensations of a different kind coming from the same point in space. So when you see a yellow color and at the same time experience a certain familiar taste and a certain softness of touch, all arising from the same source, then by a series of classifying judgments you put all these different sensations together, assign them to the same object, and give that object a name--for example, "butter."

[Sidenote: The Archives of the Mind]

This process of grouping and classification that we are describing under the name of "classifying judgments" is no haphazard affair. It is carried on in strict compliance with certain well-defined laws.

These laws prescribe and determine the workings of your mind just as absolutely as the laws of physics control the operations of material forces.

While each of these laws has its own special province and jurisdiction, yet all have one element in common, and that is that they all relate to those mental operations by which sense-perceptions, causal judgments, and even classifying judgments, past, present and imaginative, are grouped, bound together, arranged, catalogued and pigeonholed in the archives of the mind.

These laws, taken collectively, are therefore called the Laws of Association.

CHAPTER IV

THE FOUR PRIME LAWS OF ASSOCIATION

[Sidenote: The Seeming Chaos of Mind]

If there is any one thing in the world that seems utterly chaotic, it is the way in which the mind wanders from one subject of thought to another. It requires but a moment for it to flash from New York to San Francisco, from San Francisco to Tokio, and around the globe. Yet mental processes are as law-abiding as anything else in Nature.

[Sidenote: Predicting Your Next Idea]

So much is this true, that if we knew every detail of your past experience from your first infantile sensation, and knew also just what you are thinking of at the present moment, we could predict to a mathematical certainty just what ideas would next appear on the kaleidoscopic screen of your thoughts. This is due to laws that govern the association of ideas.

These laws are, in substance, that the way in which judgments and ideas are classified and stored away, and the order in which they are brought forth into consciousness depends upon what other judgments and ideas they have been associated with most habitually, recently, closely and vividly.

There are, therefore, four Prime Laws of Association--the Law of Habit, the Law of Recency, the Law of Contiguity and the Law of Vividness.

Every idea that can possibly arise in your thoughts has its vast array of associates, to each of which it is linked by some one element in common. Thus, you see or dream of a yellow flower, and the one property of yellowness links the idea of that flower with everything you ever before saw or dreamed of that was similarly hued.

[Sidenote: The Bonds of Intellect]

But the yellow-flower thought is not tied to all these countless associates by bonds of equal strength. And which associate shall come next to mind is determined by the four Prime Laws of Association.

The Law of Habit requires that frequency of association be the one test to determine what idea shall next come into consciousness, while the Laws of Recency, Contiguity and Vividness emphasize respectively recency of occurrence, closeness in point of space and intensity of impression. Which law and which element shall prevail is all a question of degree.

The most important of these laws is the Law of Habit. In obedience to this law, the next idea to enter the mind will be the one that has been most frequently associated with the interesting part of the subject you are now thinking of.

The sight of a pile of manuscript on your desk ready for the printer, the thought of a printer, the word "printer," spoken or printed, calls to mind the particular printer with whom you have been dealing for some years.

The word "cocoa," the thought of a cup of cocoa, the mental picture of a cup of cocoa, may conjure with it not merely a steaming cup before the mind's eye and the flavor of the contents, but also a daintily clad figure in apron and cap bearing the brand of some well-known cocoa manufacturer.

If a typist or pianist has learned one system of fingering, it is almost impossible to change, because each letter, each note on the keyboard is associated with the idea of movement in a particular finger. Constant use has so welded these associations together that when one enters the mind it draws its associate in its train.

Test the truth of these principles for yourself. Try them out and see whether the elements of habit, contiguity, recency and intensity do not determine all questions of association.

[Sidenote: Brands and Tags]

If you wanted to buy a house, what local subdivision would come first to your mind, and why? If you were about to purchase a new tire for your automobile or a few pairs of stockings, what brand would you buy, and why? When you think of a camera or a cake of soap, what particular make comes first to your mind? When you think of a home, what is the mental picture that rises before you, and why?

Whatever the article, whether it be one of food or luxury or investment, or even of sentiment, you will find that it is tagged with a definite associate--a name, a brand, or a personality characterized by frequency, recency, closeness or vividness of presentation to your consciousness.

The grouping together of sensations into integral ideas is one step in the complicated mental processes by which useful knowledge is acquired. But the associative processes go much beyond this.

[Sidenote: How Experience is Systematized]

We also compare the different objects of present and past experience. We carefully and thoroughly catalogue them into groups, divisions and subdivisions for convenient and ready reference. This we do by the processes of memory, of association and of discrimination, previously referred to.

[Sidenote: How Language Is Simplified]

Through these processes our knowledge of the world, derived from the whole vast field of experience, is unified and systematized. Through these processes is order realized from chaos. Through these processes it comes about that not only individual thought, but the communication of thought from one person to another, is vastly simplified. Language is enabled to deal with ideas instead of with isolated sense-perceptions. The single word "horse" suffices to convey a thought that could not be adequately set forth in a page-long enumeration of disconnected sense-perceptions.

The associative process covers a wide range. It includes, for example, not only the simple definition of an aggregate of sense-perceptions, as "horse" or "cow"; it includes as well the inferential process of abstract reasoning.

[Sidenote: Processes of Reasoning and Reflection]

The only real difference between these widely diverse mental acts, one apparently so much less complicated and profound than the other, is that the former involves no act of memory, while the latter is based wholly on sensory experiences of the past.

Abstract reasoning is merely reasoning from premises and to conclusions which are not present to our senses at the time.

CHAPTER V

EMOTIONAL ENERGY IN BUSINESS

[Sidenote: Ideas that Stimulate]

It is a recognized fact of observation that Every idea has a certain emotional quality associated with it, a sort of "feeling tone."

If ideas of health and triumphant achievement are brought into consciousness, we at the same time experience a state of energy, a feeling of courage and capability and joy and a stimulation of all the bodily processes. If, on the other hand, ideas of disease and death and failure are brought into consciousness, we at the same time experience feelings of sorrow and mental suffering and a state of lethargy, a feeling of inertia, impotence and fatigue.

THE LAW

Exalted ideas have associated with them a vitalizing and energizing emotional quality. Depressive memories or ideas have associated with them a depressing and disintegrating emotional quality.

[Sidenote: Pivotal Law of Business Passion]

The wise application of this law will lead you to vigorous health and material prosperity. Its disregard or misuse brings deterioration and failure.

The distinction between wise use and misuse lies in whether disintegrating or creative thoughts, with their correspondingly energizing or depressing emotions or feelings, are allowed to hold sway in consciousness.

[Sidenote: Energizing Emotions]

When we speak of energizing emotions or feelings we mean love, courage, brightness, earnestness, cheer, enthusiasm. When we speak of depressing emotions or feelings we mean doubt, fear, worry, gloom.

No elements are more essential to a successful business or a successful life than the right kind of emotional elements. Yet they are rarely credited with the importance to which they are entitled.

To the unthinking the word "emotion" has the same relation to success that foam has to the water beneath. Yet nothing could be farther from the truth. Emotion, earnestness, fire, enthusiasm--these are the very life of effort. They are steam to the engine; they are what the lighted fuse is to the charge of dynamite. They are the elements that give flash to the eye, spring to the step, resoluteness to the languid and certainty to effort. They are the elements that distinguish the living, acting forces of achievement from the spiritless forces of failure.

[Sidenote: Cross-Roads of Success or Failure]

No man ever rose very high who did not possess strong reserves of emotional energy. Napoleon said, "I would rather have the ardor of my soldiers, and they half-trained, than have the best fighting machines in Europe without this element."

Emotional energy of the right kind makes one fearless and undaunted in the face of any discouragement. It is never at rest. It feeds on its own achievements. It is the love of an Heloise and the ambition of an Alexander.

[Sidenote: The Life of Effort]

It is this emotional energy that makes business passion, that makes men love their business, that brings their hearts into harmony with their undertakings, and that gives them splendid visions of commercial greatness.

[Sidenote: The Motive Power of Progress]

Through all the ages great souls have drowsed in spiritless acquiescence until some tide of emotional energy swept over them, "as the breeze wanders over the dead strings of some Aeolian harp, and sweeps the music which slumbers upon them now into divine murmurings, now into stormy sobs." And then, and then, these Joans of Arc, these Hermit Peters, these Abraham Lincolns, these Pierpont Morgans, these warriors, statesmen, financiers, business men, salesmen, these practical crusaders and business enthusiasts, have sent out their influence into measureless fields of achievement.

Emotional energy generated on proper lines, and based on the support of a fixed intent, is a force that nothing can withstand, and we tell you that every idea that comes into your mind has its emotional quality, and that by the intelligent direction of your conscious "thinking" you can call into your life or drive out of it these powerful emotional influences for good or evil.

[Sidenote: The Value of an Idea]

As Mr. Waldo P. Warren says, "Who can measure the value of an idea? Starting as the bud of an acorn, it becomes at last a forest of mighty oaks; or beginning as a spark it consumes the rubbish of centuries.

"Ideas are as essential to progress as a hub to a wheel, for they form the center around which all things revolve. Ideas begin great enterprises, and the workers of all lands do their bidding. Ideas govern the governors, rule the rulers, and manage the managers of all nations and industries. Ideas are the motive power which turns the tireless wheels of toil. Ideas raise the plowboy to president, and constitute the primal element of the success of men and nations. Ideas form the fire that lights the torch of progress, leading on the centuries. Ideas are the keys which open the storehouses of possibility. Ideas are the passports to the realms of great achievement. Ideas are the touch-buttons which connect the currents of energy with the wheels of history. Ideas determine the bounds, break the limits, move on the goal, and waken latent capacity to successive sunrises of better days."

Even without our telling you, you know that whenever a man makes up his mind that he is beaten in some fight his very thinking so helps on the fatal outcome.

[Sidenote: The Hard Work Required to Fail]

The truth is, It takes just as much brain work to accomplish a failure as it does to win success--just as much effort to build up a depressive mental attitude as an energizing one.

[Sidenote: Creative Power of Thought]

Take for granted that you have the courage, the energy, the self-confidence and the enthusiasm to do what you want to do, and you will find yourself in possession of these splendid qualities when the need arises.

Consciously or unconsciously, you have already trained your mind to discriminate among sense-impressions. It perceives some and ignores others. For each perception it selects such associates as you have trained it to select. Have you trained it wisely? Does it associate the new facts of observation with those memory-pictures that will make the new ideas useful and productive of fruitful bodily activities?

[Sidenote: Conscious and Unconscious Training]

If not, it is time for you to turn over a new leaf and habitually and persistently direct your attention to those associative elements in each new-learned fact that will make for health and happiness and success. Train your mind deliberately, and day by day, to such constant incorporation of feelings of courage and confidence and assurance into all your thoughts that the associated impulses to bodily activity will inevitably influence your whole life.

At the outset of every undertaking you are confronted with two ways of attacking it. One is with doubt and uncertainty; the other is with courage and confidence.

[Sidenote: Two Ways of Attacking Business Problems]

The first of these mental attitudes is purely negative. It is inhibitory. It is made up of mental pictures of yourself in direful situations, and these mental pictures bring with them depressing emotions and muscular inhibitions.

The second attitude is positive. It is inspiring. It is made up of mental pictures of yourself bringing the affair to a triumphant issue, and these mental pictures bring with them stimulating emotions and the impulses to those bodily activities that will realize your aims.

You have only to start the thing off with the right mental attitude and hold to it. All the rest is automatic. Think this over.

Put this same idea into your business. Analyze your business with reference to its mental attitude. Of course, you know all about its organization, its various departments, its machinery and equipment, its methods, its cost system, its organized efficiency. But what about its mental attitude? Every store, every industrial establishment has an air of its own, an indefinite something that distinguishes it from every other. This is why you buy your cigars at one place instead of at another.

[Sidenote: Cutting into the Quick]

Look behind the methods and the systems and all the wooden machinery of your business and you come to its throbbing life. There you find the characteristic quality that governs its future. There you find the attitude, the mental attitude, that pulls the strings determining the conduct of clerks and salesmen, managers and superintendents, and this attitude is in the last analysis a reflection of the mental attitude of the executive head himself--not necessarily the nominal executive head, but the real executive head, however he be called.

[Sidenote: Executives Real and Sham]

Does the truckman whistle at his work? Is the salesman proud of his line and his house? Does he approach his "prospect" with the confident enthusiasm that brings orders? Does the shipping clerk take a delighted interest in getting out his deliveries? They must have this mental attitude, or you will never win. Are you yourself "making good" in this respect? Remember that, whether you know it or not, your inmost thoughts are reflected in your voice and manner, your every act. And all your subordinates, whether they know it or not, see these things and reflect your attitude.

[Sidenote: Mental Attitude of One's Business]

Therefore, in all you do, and in all you think, do it and think it with courage and with unwavering faith, fearing nothing.

Later on we shall instruct you in specific methods that will enable you to follow this injunction. For the present we must be content with emphasizing its importance.

[Sidenote: Psychological Engineering]

In what follows in this book we shall bring forth no new principle of mental operation, but shall illustrate those already learned by reference to certain practical uses to which they can be applied. Our purpose in this is to impress you with the immense practical value of the knowledge you are acquiring, and to show you that this course of reading has nothing to do with telepathy, spiritism, clairvoyance, animal magnetism, fortune-telling, astrology or witchcraft, but, on the contrary, that in its revelation of mental principles and processes it is laying a scientific basis for a highly differentiated type of efficiency engineering.

CHAPTER VI

HOW TO SELECT EMPLOYEES

In the preceding volume, entitled "Making Your Own World," you learned that reaction-time is the interval that elapses between the moment when a sense-vibration reaches the body and the moment when perception is made known by some outward response.

[Sidenote: A Clue to Adaptability]

Reaction-time can be made to furnish a clue to the adaptability of the individual for any business, profession or vocation.

To determine the character, accuracy and rapidity of the mental reactions of different individuals under different conditions, various scientific methods have been evolved and cunning devices invented.

[Sidenote: Mapping the Mentality]

There are decisive reaction-time tests by which you may readily map out your own mentality or that of any other person, including, for instance, those who may seek employment under you.

Have you been harboring the delusion that "quick as thought" is a phrase expressive of flash-like quickness? Have you had the idea that thought is instantaneous? If so, you must alter your conceptions.

The fact is that your merely automatic reactions from sense-impressions can be measured in tenths of a second, while a really intellectual operation of the simplest character requires from one to several seconds.

An important thing for you to know in this connection is that no two people are alike in this respect. Some think quickly along certain lines; some along other lines.

[Sidenote: The Kind of "Help" You Need]

And the man or woman that you need in any department of your business is that one whose mind works swiftly in the particular way required for your business.

How rapidly does your mind work? How fast do your thoughts come, compared to the average man in your field of activity?

How fast does your stenographer think? Your clerk? Your chauffeur? Are they up to the average of those engaged in similar work? If not, you had best make a change.

[Sidenote: Tests for Different Mental Traits]

A large number of tests and mechanical devices, some of them most complicated, have been scientifically formulated or invented to measure the quickness of different kinds of mental operations in the individual.

One very simple test which we give merely to illustrate the principle is called the "Test of Uncontrolled Association." All the materials needed for this test are a stop-watch and a blank form containing numbered spaces for one hundred words.

[Sidenote: Test of Uncontrolled Associations]

Give these instructions to the person you are examining: "When I say 'Now!' I want you to start in with some word, any one you like, and keep on saying words as fast as you can until you have given a hundred different words. You may give any words you like, but they must not be in sentences. I will tell you when to stop." You then start your stop-watch with the command "Now!" and write the words on the blank form as fast as they are spoken. Mere abbreviations or shorthand will suffice. When the hundredth word is reached, stop the watch and note the time.

The average time for lists of words written in this fashion is about 308 seconds.

[Sidenote: Test for Quick Thinking]

This is a fair test of the rapidity of the associative processes of the mind. It will reveal many strange and characteristic idiosyncrasies. On the other hand, considering the vast number of words available, it is remarkable to note the degree of community to be found in the words that will be given by a number of persons. Thus, "in fifty lists (5,000 words) only 2,024 words were different, only 1,266 occurred but once, while the one hundred most frequent words made up three-tenths of the whole number."

Professor Jastrow, of Wisconsin University, has found also that the "class to which women contribute most largely is that of articles of dress, one word in every eleven belonging to this class. The inference from this, that dress is the predominant category of the feminine (or of the privy feminine) mind, is valid, with proper reservations."

[Sidenote: Measuring Speed of Thought]

Another method of testing speed of thought is to pronounce a series of words and after each word have the subject speak the first word that comes to him. The answers are taken down and are timed with a stop-watch. About the quickest answers by an alert person will be made in one second, or one and one-fifth seconds, while most persons take from one and three-fifths to two and three-fifths seconds to answer, under the most favorable circumstances. Puzzling words or conflicting emotions will prolong this time to five and ten seconds in many cases. Much depends upon the kind of words propounded to the subject, starting with such simple words as "hat" and "coat," and changing to words that tend to arouse emotion. A list of words may be carefully selected to fit the requirements of different classes of subjects.

[Sidenote: Range of Mental Tests]

By appropriate tests, the quickness of response to sense-impressions, the character of the associations of ideas, the workings of the individual imagination, the nature of the emotional tendencies, the character and scope of the powers of attention and discrimination, the degree of persistence of the individual and his susceptibility to fatigue in certain forms of effort, the visual, auditory and manual skill, and even the moral character of the subject, can be more or less clearly and definitely determined.

It is possible by these tests to distinguish individual differences in thought processes as conditioned by age, sex, training, physical condition, and so on, to analyze the comparative mental efficiency of the worker at different periods in the day's work as affected by long hours of application, by monotony and variety of occupation and the like, and even to reveal obscure mental tendencies and to disclose motives or information that are being intentionally concealed.

[Sidenote: Tests for Army and Navy]

Among the simplest of such tests are those for vision, hearing and color discrimination. Tests of this kind are now given to all applicants for enlistment in the army, the navy and the marine corps, and more exacting tests of the same sort are given to candidates for licenses as pilots and for positions as officers of ships.

[Sidenote: Tests for Railroad Employees]

Employees of railroads, and in some cases those of street railroads, also, are subjected to tests for vision, hearing and color-discrimination. In the case of trainmen the color-discrimination tests result in the rejection of about four per cent of the applicants. The tests are repeated every two years for all the men and at intervals of six months for those suspected of defects in color discrimination. In all of these cases the tests have for their object the detection and rejection of unfit applicants.

[Sidenote: What One Factory Saved]

One of the earliest instances of work of this kind was the introduction a few years ago of reaction-time tests in selecting girls for the work of inspecting for flaws the steel balls used in ball bearings. This work requires a concentrated type of attention, good visual acuity and quick and keen perception, accompanied by quick responsive action. The scientific investigator went into a bicycle ball factory and with a stop-watch measured the reaction-time of all the girls then at work. All those who showed a long time between stimulus and reaction-time were then eliminated. The final outcome was that thirty-five girls did the work formerly done by one hundred and twenty; the accuracy of the work was increased by sixty-six per cent; the wages of the girls were doubled; the working day was shortened from ten and one-half hours to eight and one-half hours; and the profit of the factory was substantially increased.

[Sidenote: Professor Musterberg's Experiments]

To illustrate the methods employed and the importance of work of this kind, we quote the following from the recent ground-breaking book, "Psychology and Industrial Efficiency," by Professor Hugo Musterberg, of Harvard University. This extract is an account of Professor Musterberg's experimental method for determining in advance the mental fitness of persons applying for positions as telephone operators. Such information would be of immense value to telephone companies, as each candidate who satisfies formal entrance requirements receives several months' training in a telephone school and is paid a salary while she is being trained.

[Sidenote: Tests for Hiring Telephone Girls]

One company alone employs twenty-three thousand operators, and more than one-third of those employed and trained at the company's expense prove unfitted and leave within six months, with a heavy resulting financial loss to the company. The tests are numerous and somewhat complicated and require more time to conduct them than tests in other lines of work, but for these very reasons will be particularly illuminating. Professor Musterberg says:

"After carefully observing the service in the central office for a while, I came to the conviction that it would not be appropriate here to reproduce the activity at the switchboard in the experiment, but that it would be more desirable to resolve that whole function into its elements and to undertake the experimental test of a whole series of elementary mental dispositions. Every one of these mental acts can then be examined according to well-known laboratory methods without giving to the experiments any direct relation to the characteristic telephone operation as such. I carried on the first series of experiments with about thirty young women who a short time before had entered into the telephone training-school, where they are admitted only at the age between seventeen and twenty-three years. I examined them with reference to eight different psychological functions. * * * A part of the psychological tests were carried on in individual examinations, but the greater part with the whole class together.

[Sidenote: Memory Test]

[Sidenote: Test for Attention]

"These common tests referred to memory, attention, intelligence, exactitude and rapidity. I may characterize the experiments in a few words. The memory examination consisted of reading the whole class at first two numbers of four digits, then two of five digits, then two of six digits, and so on up to figures of twelve digits, and demanding that they be written down as soon as a signal was given. The experiments on attention, which in this case of the telephone operators seemed to me especially significant, made use of a method the principle of which has frequently been applied in the experimental psychology of individual differences, and which I adjusted to our special needs. The requirement is to cross out a particular letter in a connected text. Every one of the thirty women in the classroom received the same first page of a newspaper of that morning. I emphasize that it was a new paper, as the newness of the content was to secure the desired distraction of the attention. As soon as the signal was given, each one of the girls had to cross out with a pencil every 'a' in the text for six minutes. After a certain time, a bell signal was given, and each then had to begin a new column. In this way we could find out, first, how many letters were correctly crossed out in those six minutes; secondly, how many letters were overlooked; and thirdly, how the recognition and the oversight were distributed in the various parts of the text. In every one of these three directions strong individual differences were indeed noticeable. Some persons crossed out many, but also overlooked many; others overlooked hardly any of the 'a's,' but proceeded very slowly, so that the total number of the crossed-out letters was small. Moreover, it was found that some at first do poor work, but soon reach a point at which their attention remains on a high level; others begin with a relatively high achievement, but after a short time their attention flags, and the number of crossed-out letters becomes smaller or the number of unnoticed, overlooked letters increases. Fluctuations of attention, deficiencies and strong points can be discovered in much detail.

[Sidenote: Test for General Intelligence]

"The third test, which was tried with the whole class, referred to the intelligence of the individuals. * * * The psychological experiments carried on in the schoolroom have demonstrated that this ability can be tested by the measurement of some very simple mental activities. * * * Among the various proposed schemes for this purpose, the figures suggest that the most reliable one is the following method, the results of which show the highest agreement between the rank order based on the experiments and the rank order of the teachers. The experiment consists in reading to the pupils a long series of pairs of words of which the two members of the pair always logically belong together. Later, one word of each pair will be read to them and they have to write down the word which belonged with it in the pair." (For example, "thunder" and "lightning" are words that "logically belong together," while "horse" and "bricks" are unrelated terms.--Editor's note.)

"This is not a simple experiment on memory. The tests have shown that if, instead of logically connected words, simply disconnected chance words are offered and reproduced, no one can keep such a long series of pairs in mind, while with the words which have related meaning, the most intelligent pupils can master the whole series. The very favorable results which this method had yielded in the classroom made me decide to try it in this case, too. I chose for an experiment twenty-four pairs of words from the sphere of experience of the girls to be tested." (For instance, "door, house"; "pillow, bed"; "letter, word"; "leaf, tree"; "button, dress"; "nose, face"; "cover, kettle"; "page, book"; "engine, train"; "glass, window"; "enemy, friend"; "telephone, bell"; "thunder, lightning"; "ice, cold"; "ink, pen"; "husband, wife"; "fire, burn"; "sorry, sad"; "well, strong"; "mother, child"; "run, fast"; "black, white"; "war, peace"; "arm, hand."--Editor's note.)

[Sidenote: Test for Exactitude]

"Two class experiments belonged rather to the periphery of psychology.

"The exactitude of space-perceptions was measured by demanding that each divide first the long and then the short edge of a folio sheet into two equal halves by a pencil-mark.

[Sidenote: Test for Rapidity of Movement]

"And finally, to measure the rapidity of movement, it was demanded that every one make with a pencil on the paper zigzag movements of a particular size during the ten seconds from one signal to another.

"After these class experiments, I turned to individual tests.

"First, every girl had to sort a pack of forty-eight cards into four piles as quickly as possible. The time was measured in fifths of a second, with an ordinary stop-watch.

[Sidenote: Test for Accuracy of Movement]

"The following experiment which referred to the accuracy of movement impulses demanded that every one try to reach with the point of a pencil three different points on the table in the rhythm of metronome beats. On each of these three places a sheet of paper was fixed with a fine cross in the middle. The pencil should hit the crossing point, and the marks on the paper indicated how far the movement had fallen short of the goal. One of these movements demanded the full extension of the arm and the other two had to be made with half-bent arm. I introduced this last test because the hitting of the right holes in the switchboard of the telephone office is of great importance.

[Illustration: TESTING STEADINESS OF MOTOR CONTROL--INVOLUNTARY MOVEMENT PRIVATE LABORATORY, SOCIETY OF APPLIED PSYCHOLOGY]

"The last individual experiment was an association test. I called six words, like 'book,' 'house,' 'rain,' and had them speak the first word which came to their minds. The time was measured in fifths of a second only, with an ordinary stop-watch, as subtler experiments, for which hundredths of a second would have to be considered, were not needed.

[Sidenote: Results of Experiments]

"In studying the results, so far as the memory experiments were concerned, we found that it would be useless to consider the figures with more than ten digits. We took the results only of those with eight, nine and ten digits. There were fifty-four possibilities of mistakes. The smallest number of actual mistakes was two, the largest twenty-nine. In the experiment on attention made with the crossing-out of letters, we found that the smallest number of correctly marked letters was 107, the largest number in the six minutes, 272; the smallest number of overlooked letters was two, the largest 135; but this last case of abnormal carelessness stood quite isolated. On the whole, the number of overlooked letters fluctuated between five and sixty. If both results, those of the crossed-out and those of the overlooked letters, are brought into relations, we find that the best results were a case of 236 letters marked, with only two overlooked, and one of 257 marked, with four overlooked. The very interesting details as to the various types of attention which we see in the distribution of mistakes over the six minutes were not taken into our final table. The word experiments by which we tested the intelligence showed that no one was able to reproduce more than twenty-two of the twenty-four words. The smallest number of words remembered was seven.

"The mistakes in the perception of distances fluctuated between one and fourteen millimeters; the time for the sorting of the forty-eight cards, between thirty-five and fifty-eight seconds; the association-time for the six associated words taken together was between nine and twenty-one seconds. The pointing experiments could not be made use of in this first series, as it was found that quite a number of participants were unable to perform the act with the rapidity demanded.

"Several ways were open to make mathematical use of these results. I preferred the simplest way. I calculated the grade of the girls for each of these achievements. The same candidate who stood in the seventh place in the memory experiment was in the fifteenth place with reference to the number of letters marked, in the third place with reference to the letters overlooked, in the twenty-first place with reference to the number of word pairs which she had grasped, in the eleventh place with reference to the exactitude of space-perception, in the sixteenth place with reference to the association-time, and in the sixth place with reference to the time of sorting. As soon as we had all these independent grades, we calculated the average and in this way ultimately gained a common order of grading. * * *

"With this average rank list, we compared the practical results of the telephone company after three months had passed. These three months had been sufficient to secure at least a certain discrimination between the best, the average, and the unfit. The result of this comparison was on the whole satisfactory. First, the skeptical telephone company had mixed with the class a number of women who had been in the service for a long while, and had even been selected as teachers in the telephone school. I did not know, in figuring out the results, which of the participants in the experiments these particularly gifted outsiders were. If the psychological experiments had brought the result that these individuals who stood so high in the estimation of the telephone company ranked low in the laboratory experiment, it would have reflected strongly on the reliability of the laboratory method. The results showed, on the contrary, that these women who had proved most able in practical service stood at the top of our list. Correspondingly, those who stood the lowest in our psychological rank list had in the mean time been found unfit in practical service, and had either left the company of their own accord or else had been eliminated. The agreement, to be sure, was not a perfect one. One of the list of women stood rather low in the psychological list, while the office reported that so far she had done fair work in the service, and two others, to whom the psychological laboratory gave a good testimonial were considered by the telephone office as only fair.

[Sidenote: Theory and Practice]

"But it is evident that certain disagreements would have occurred even with a more ideal method, as on the one side no final achievement in practical service can be given after only three months, and because on the other side a large number of secondary factors may enter which entirely overshadow the mere question of psychological fitness. Poor health, for instance, may hinder even the most fit individual from doing satisfactory work, and extreme industry and energetic will may for a while lead even the unfit to fair achievement, which, to be sure, is likely to be coupled with a dangerous exhaustion. The slight disagreements between the psychological results and the practical valuation, therefore, do not in the least speak against the significance of such a method. On the other hand, I emphasize that this first series meant only the beginning of the investigation, and it can hardly be expected that at such a first approach the best and most suitable methods would at once be hit upon. A continuation of the work will surely lead to much better combinations of test experiments and to better adjusted schemes."

[Sidenote: How to Identify the Unfit]

Analytical test studies such as the foregoing form an almost infallible means for finding out the unfit at the very beginning instead of after a long and costly experimental trying-out in vocational training-school or in actual service.

Whatever your line of business may be, you may rest assured that an analysis of its needs will disclose numerous departments in which specific mental tests and devices may be employed with a great saving in time and money and a vastly increased efficiency and output of working energy.

[Sidenote: Means to Great Business Economies]

Suppose that you are the manager of a street railroad employing a large number of motormen. Would it not be of the greatest value to you if in a few moments you could determine in advance whether any given applicant for a position possessed the quickness of response to danger signals that would enable him to avoid accidents? Think what this would mean to the profits of your company in cutting down the number of damage claims arising from accidents! Some electric railroad companies have as many as fifty thousand accident indemnity cases per year, which involve an expense amounting in some cases to thirteen per cent of the annual gross earnings. Yet a comparatively simple mechanism has been devised for determining by the reaction-time of any applicant whether he would or would not be quick enough to stop his car if a child ran in front of its wheels.

[Sidenote: Round Pegs in Square Holes]

The general employment of this test would result in the rejection of about twenty-five per cent of those who are now employed as motormen with a correspondingly large reduction in the number of deaths and injuries from street-car accidents. And on the other hand, the general use of psychological tests in other lines of work would make room for these men in places for which they are peculiarly adapted and where their earning power would be greater.

If, for example, the applicant responds to the signs of an emergency in three-fifths of a second or less, and has the mental characteristics that will enable him at the same time to maintain the speed required by the schedule, he may be mentally fitted for the "job" of motorman; while if it takes him one second or more to act in an emergency, he may be a dangerous man for the company and for the public.

[Sidenote: The Danger in Two-Fifths of a Second]

Two-fifths of a second difference in time-reactions may mark the line between safety and disaster. How absurd it is to trust to luck in matters of this kind when by means of scientific experimental tests you can accurately gauge your man before he has a chance to involve you or your company in a heartbreaking tragedy and serious financial loss!

You can readily see that very similar tests could be devised to meet the needs of the employer of chauffeurs, as, for example, the manager of a taxicab company, or the requirements of a railroad in the hiring of its engineers.

[Sidenote: Picking a Private Secretary]

You should not employ as private secretary a person whose reactions indicate a natural inability to keep a secret. This quality of mind can be simply and unerringly detected by psychological tests.

[Sidenote: Finding Out the Close-Mouthed]

One quality entering into the ability to keep a secret is the degree of suggestibility of the individual. That person who most quickly and automatically obeys and responds to suggested commands possesses the least degree of conscious self-control. The quality referred to is illustrated by the child's game of "thumbs up, thumbs down," and "Simon says thumbs up" and "Simon says thumbs down." Those persons who are unable to wait for the "Simon says," but mechanically obey the command "thumbs up" or "thumbs down" would be those least able to resist a trap artfully laid to compel them to disclose what they wished to conceal. Like efficiency in observation, attention and memory, however, suggestibility is specific, not general, in character--that is to say, persons may be easily influenced by certain kinds of suggestion while possessing a strong degree of resistance to other kinds. Consequently actual tests of this quality cannot be limited to one method.

For purposes of illustration, here is a simple form of what is known as the "line" test for suggestibility. The subject is seated about two feet away from and in front of a revolving drum on which is a strip of white paper. On this strip of white paper are drawn twenty parallel straight lines. These lines begin at varying distances from the left-hand margin. Each of the first four lines is fifty per cent longer than the one before it, but the remaining sixteen lines are all of the same length.

[Sidenote: A Test for Suggestibility]

The examiner says to the subject, "I want to see how good your 'eye' is. I'll show you a line, say an inch or two long, and I want you to reproduce it right afterwards from memory. Some persons make bad mistakes; they may make a line two inches long when I show them one three inches long; others make one four or five inches long. Let's see how well you can do. I shall show you the line through this slit. Take just one look at it, then make a mark on this paper [cross-section paper] just the distance from this left-hand margin that the line is long. Do that with each line as it appears."

The lines are then shown one at a time, and after each is noted it is turned out of sight. As the lines of equal length are presented, the examiner says alternately, "Here is a longer one," "Here is a shorter one," and so on. The extent to which these misleading suggestions of the examiner are accepted and acted upon by the subject in plain violation of the evidence of his senses tests in a measure his suggestibility, his automatic, mechanical and immediate responsiveness to the influence of others and his comparative lack of strong resistance to such outside influences. Inability to satisfactorily meet this and similar tests for suggestibility would indicate an unfitness for such duties as those required by a private secretary, who must at all times have himself well in hand and not be easily lured into embarrassing revelations.

[Sidenote: Selecting a Stenographer]

You should not employ as stenographer a person whose time-reactions indicate a slowness of auditory response or an inability to carry in mind a long series of dictated words, or whose vocabulary is too limited for the requirements of your business.

[Sidenote: Tests for Auditory Acuity]

The quickness of auditory response may be determined either by speech tests or by instrumental tests. In either case the acuteness of hearing of the applicant is measured by the ability to promptly and correctly report sounds at various known ranges, the acuity of the normal ear under precisely similar conditions having been previously determined. Speech involves a great variety of combinations--of pitch, accent, inflection and emphasis. Consequently a scientific speech test involves the preparation of lists of words based upon an analysis of the elements of whispered and spoken utterance. This work has been done, and such lists and tests are available.

[Sidenote: A Test for Rote Memory]

For testing the ability to remember a series of dictated words the following lists of words are recommended:

Concrete Abstract Concrete Abstract Concrete Abstract

street scope coat time pen law ink proof woman aft clock thought lamp scheme house route man plot spoon form salt phase floor glee horse craft glove work sponge life chair myth watch truth hat rhythm stone rate box thing chalk faith ground cause mat tact knife mirth

The examiner should repeat these lists of words to the subject one at a time, alternating the concrete and abstract lists. To insure the presentation of the words with an even tempo, a metronome may be had by simply swinging a small weight on a string, having the string of just sufficient length so that the beats come at intervals of one second. Each word should be pronounced distinctly in time with the beat of the metronome, but without rhythm. After each list has been pronounced, have the subject write the list from memory. The lists thus made up by the subject from memory are then to be inspected with reference to the following points:

1. Memory errors (omissions and displacements), concrete lists.

2. Memory errors (omissions and displacements), abstract lists.

Every omission counts two errors; every displacement counts two-thirds when the displacement is by one remove only, one and one-third when by more than one move.

3. Insertions. These are words added by the subject. They count for two errors each, unless the added word resembles the word given in sound, in which case it counts one and one-third.

4. Perseverations. These are reproductions in a given series of words already given in a previous series. If frequent, this indicates a low order of intelligence, with weak self-control and poor critical judgment. Each perseveration counts four.

5. Substitution of synonyms, when a word of like meaning but different sound is substituted for the word given; counts one and one-third.

[Sidenote: A Test for Range of Vocabulary]

An approximate determination of the range of vocabulary of your prospective stenographer can be had by the use of the following comparatively short and simple test.

Hand the applicant a printed slip bearing the list of one hundred words given here and ask him to mark the words carefully according to these instructions.

Place before each word one of these three signs:

(I) A plus sign (+) if you know the word.

(II) A minus sign (-) if you do not know the word.

(III) A question mark (?) if you are in doubt.

When you have finished, count the marks and fill out these blanks, making sure that the numbers add to one hundred.

Number known ....

Number unknown ....

Number doubtful ....

abductor decide interim rejoice abeam deception lanuginose rejoin abed disentomb lanuginous rejoinder abet disentrance lanugo rejuvenate amalgamation disepalous lanyard scroll amanuensis disestablish matting scrub amaranth eschar mattock scruff baron escheat mattress scrunch baroscope escort maturate skylight barouche eschalot muff skyrocket barque filiform muffin skysail bottle-holder filigree muffle skyward bottom filing mufti subcutaneous bottomry fill page sub-let boudoir gourd pagoda subdue channel gout paid tenderloin chant govern pail tendinous chanticleer gown photograph tendon chaos hodman photographer tendril concatenate hoe photography tycoon concatenation hoecake photo-lithograph tymbal concave hog publication type conceal intercede pudding virago decemvirate interdict puddle virescent decency interest pudgy virgin

By adding find the total number of "plus" marks on the applicant's slip. Multiply this number by 280, and you will then have obtained the applicant's absolute vocabulary.

An absolute vocabulary of twenty thousand words or over may be graded as excellent; 17,500 to 20,000 words, good; 15,000 to 17,500, fair; and below 15,000, poor.

You should not employ as train-dispatcher a person whose time-reactions indicate a tendency to confuse associated ideas. The associated ideas may be related in time, place or a variety of ways, and the memory of one who has an inherent tendency to substitute an associate for the thing itself is a treacherous instrument. The tendency to confuse associated ideas can be measured by psychological tests.

Your own knowledge of the work of the world will suggest other employments besides that of train-dispatcher in which such a test could be used in hiring men to the improvement of the service.

[Sidenote: Crime-Detection by Psychological Tests]

The employment of psychological tests in the detection of crime is fast supplanting the brutalities of the "third degree."

Thus, for example, by the use of highly sensitive instruments we are able to detect the quickened heart-beat, the shudder, and other evidences of emotion not otherwise discernible, but due to the deliberate presentation of the details and evidences of a crime. Though the subject may not himself be aware of the slightest physical expression of emotion, these signs of a disturbed mentality are unerringly revealed by the delicate instruments of the psychologist.

[Sidenote: The Factory Operative's Attention Power]

In some factories the operative is called upon to simultaneously keep watch over a large number of parts of a moving mechanism, and to note and quickly correct a disturbance in any part. Eye and ear must have a wide range, must be able to take account of a large number of operations widely separated in space.

For the scientific determination of the operative's range of visual attention, the "disc tachistoscope," shown facing page 106, may be used. This is a form of short-exposure apparatus. The essential idea is to furnish a field upon which the subject may for a moment fasten his attention, and then to substitute for this field another containing certain prepared test-material. This last field is exposed for but a brief instant and removed, and the subject is then called upon to report all that he has seen during the last exposure. Tests of this kind have demonstrated that the range of visual attention is a comparatively constant quantity with each individual, having but little relation to general ability or intelligence and being but little affected by practice.

It matters not how painstaking the individual may be, he will fail in a test of this kind and at work of this kind if the type of attention that Nature gave him is unfitted for such an "expanded" watchfulness. Yet in any type of work requiring a focusing of the attention upon a minute operation so as to note nice discriminations and detect subtle differences, he might prove a most excellent worker.

[Sidenote: Kinds of Testing Apparatus]

The kind of apparatus, the method to be employed and the place for the experiment are all matters that vary with the conditions of the special problem. The apparatus may be simple and easily devised, or it may be intricate and the result of years of investigation and a large expenditure of money.

If there seems to you to be anything impracticable in the employment of tests in the manner we have indicated, please remember that for many years those seeking employment as railroad engineers have been required to pass tests for color-blindness, tests just as truly psychological as any that we have here referred to and differing from them only in respect to the character and complexity of the qualities tested.

[Sidenote: Analysis of Different Callings]

Every calling can be analyzed and the mental elements requisite for success in that particular line can be scientifically disentangled. Methods for testing the individual as to his possession of any one or all of the mental elements required in any given vocation may then be devised in the psychological laboratory.

Furthermore, definite and scientific exercises can be formulated whereby the individual may train and develop special senses, faculties and powers so as the better to fit himself for his chosen field of work.

[Sidenote: Exercises for Developing Special Faculties]

The use of the experimental method is new to every department of science. Crude and occasional experiments have marked the advance of physics, physiology and chemistry, but it is only with the recent innovation of the scientific laboratory that these sciences have made their greatest strides.

The employment of this method in dealing with problems of the mind is particularly new. So far as we are aware there is no school in all the world that employs definite and scientific exercises in the discipline and training of its pupils in power of observation, imagination and memory.

You have now completed a brief survey of the fundamental processes of the mind and seen something of the practical utility of this knowledge. You have before you "sense-perceptions," "causal judgments," "classifying judgments," and "associated emotional qualities" or "feeling tones." Every suggested idea, every act of reasoning is in the last analysis the product of one or more of these elementary forms of mental activity.

We shall now go on to consider the operations of these mental processes in connection with certain mental phenomena.

[Sidenote: Principles that Bear on Practical Affairs]

Our purpose in all this is not to teach you the elements of psychology as it is ordinarily conceived or taught. Our aim is to conduct you through certain special fields of psychological investigation, fields that within the past few years have produced remarkable discoveries of which the world, outside of a few specialists, knows little or nothing. In this way you will be fitted to comprehend the practical instruction, the application of these principles to practical affairs, toward which this Course is tending.

###

www.ingramcontent.com/pod-product-compliance
Lightning Source LLC
Chambersburg PA
CBHW072049190526
45165CB00019B/2226